Giving Up Mediocrity

A 40-Day Fast Toward Living a Crazy Fulfilled Life

TIA NORMAN

Copyright ©2018 Tia Norman

All Rights Reserved

ISBN-13: 978-1985025912
ISBN-10: 1985025914

For my son, John & my daughter, Kennedy

I hope you always accept the invitation.

And my mom

who has always supported my dreams.

CONTENTS

Acknowledgments

Why Keep the Chocolate?   2

Lent   6

Mediocre   7

Full   8

I am "they"   9

Day 1 to 40   10 - 49

ACKNOWLEDGMENTS

Thank you to my friends, my family and the dreamers at Awakenings Movement who are making the world a better place. Rebecca, your invitation during a time of great frustration changed my life. Brian, little did we know you were snapping a picture for a book cover that day in March – thank you.

Marlon and Danielle, you have helped me look up from the mud and see beauty in the walls of the parting sea.

Why Keep the Chocolate?

As someone who was not raised in an environment that involved many religious traditions connected to a church community and who is now deeply involved in exploring, discovering and leading in such a community, there are times when I feel like I am learning backward.

Here's a specific example of what learning backward has looked like for me. The traditions surrounding Lent are fairly newer to me than to others who were raised in certain Christian settings. I find value in honoring this time, and it also sparks a lot of curiosity for me. Years ago I decided it was a custom that I'd participate in, and I relied heavily on how I saw others participating in order to figure out what I'd give up. I found myself wrestling with the question, "What does a beginner give up for Lent?"

The answer: Chocolate. (Of which I am a big fan.)

It was a bit of a challenge and involved a lot of self-talk and internal prodding and pleading as to why I should not give in to the temptation to have at least one taste of the sweet treat during the fast.

I managed to make it through the 40 days successfully. I don't really know what big revelations or transformation I expected to come as a result of this ritual of chocolate sacrifice and prayer, and in hindsight that may explain why there were none.

Several years passed and I continued, beginning each Ash Wednesday, to give up something that I had a strong desire for, and looked forward to Resurrection Sunday when I could give in to what I gave up.

Then March 1, 2017 rolled around. A Wednesday. An Ash Wednesday to be exact. A Wednesday that started with completing a presentation for a meeting the following day. The meeting was set with executives from the marketing agency I was working for and a client our team had collectively managed a Super Bowl LI project for. I knew when that meeting ended I would no longer have a job. It was a decision that had been made in October of the previous year. This was my last project, my last client. There was no new position in the pipeline. The thought of what was next made me anxious. The thought of looking for something that could very well have me end up back in a similar situation made my stomach ache.

    For the first time in nearly 23 years of working and providing for myself and my family, I was about to be officially unemployed. This was a day when I not only needed chocolate; I needed to give myself permission to explore what life outside of corporate America might hold for me. Instead of giving in to my fear and anxiety, I needed to celebrate. I immediately realized there was a place I could do both – and so I drove to Crumbville, Texas.

    Crumbville is the home of the storefront of F-dub-a-licious Treats, where my friend Ella Russell sells cookies and her signature cupcakes called Stuffed Cups. She started her business in her home over a decade ago and eventually left corporate America to grow it. It was clear that my celebration had to begin with a Stuffed Cup, and it needed to include sitting inside someone else's dream that had become a reality as reassurance that I would be okay.

    It was there in her storefront that I decided that for the next 39 days I would give up looking for my next title, keep the chocolate, and dedicate my time to making my own dreams a reality.

My intention with the content that you'll find in the pages and days ahead is to share my best effort at condensing my self-talk during the past 11 months, as they have served as a time of great discovery and practice of diving into what is sweet and giving up mediocrity.

A practice in which I must continuously remind myself that I am only limited by my thoughts and beliefs and am worthy of accepting the invitation to live life to the full.

Tia Norman
February 2, 2018

Lent

lent/

noun

noun: Lent

the period preceding Easter that in the Christian Church is devoted to fasting, abstinence, and penitence in commemoration of Christ's fasting in the wilderness. In the Western Church, it runs from Ash Wednesday to Holy Saturday and so includes forty weekdays.

me·di·o·cre

mēdēˈōkər/

adjective

of only moderate quality; not very good.

full

fu̇l

adjective

1. containing or holding as much or as many as possible; having no empty space.

2. not lacking or omitting anything; complete.

"The thief comes only to steal and kill and destroy; I have come that they may have life, and have it to the full."

John 10:10

Day 1

Listen to the voices in your head, the tug in your gut, the ache in your heart that says, "There has to be more to life than this." Know that there is. Today, give up the urge to quiet your inner voice.

Day 2

Keep it to yourself. Your dream is your dream. Be selective about who you share your visions with. If your visions were for someone else they would not have been given to you. Some things are meant to be kept between you and your Creator. Today, give up the urge to tell everyone everything.

Day 3

You do not need permission to follow your heart and the life you desire. The call is the permission. The voices on the outside may be louder than your inner voice. Today, learn to listen to and trust that still-small voice, and give up listening to voices that distract.

Day 4

Things may not go the way you want them to go. They will go the way they are supposed to go. There are no mistakes. There are only opportunities to learn and get clearer about what we want. Today, learn, gain clarity, give up the word "mistake" and know that nothing is wasted.

Day 5

Let go of a title. The thing that you're here to do might not fit into the current list of available professional titles. Stop obsessing over what you'll call yourself. Today, do the work and trust that the perfect title will find you later. Give up the need to be known by anything other than your name.

Day 6

Give up the noise. Be still. Be quiet. Today, give up 10 minutes of your busy schedule and spend it in complete silence, with no interruptions. Use a timer. Close your eyes and breathe. What do you hear? What do you smell? How do you feel? Did time drag on or did it go by fast? What was it like to sit with yourself? What did you learn?

Day 7

Give up focusing on the past. Give up fast forwarding to tomorrow. Today, be present.

Day 8

Give up operating from a cup that's half full. Today, commit to listening to your body and begin building rest into your schedule.

Day 9

Everything doesn't have to be done right now. When our to-do lists are long, our mind is setting our body up for disappointment. What one thing can you do well today and be proud of? Today, give up the urge to measure your worthiness by the number of tasks you complete. Do one thing. Do it well and hold the rest of the list loosely.

Day 10

Learn something from someone who has blazed a trail you want to follow. Who do you admire? Who is putting work out into the world that you can imagine yourself doing? Today, find at least one thing that will educate you on how your dream can become reality, and give up the notion that this is "just the way it is."

Day 11

Remind fear and anxiety that you've all met before and that this time around their participation is not needed. Give up giving in to emotions that keep you from moving ahead.

Day 12

You were not designed to shrink, to be small and for your gifts to go unnoticed. You were designed to live a big, bold life. Today, give yourself permission to move confidently in the direction of your dreams, and give up taking up less space.

Day 13

Practice saying no. Today, decline something that you truly don't want to do. Say no. Add a thank you if you'd like. Today, give up people pleasing, and make "no" a complete sentence.

Day 14

Write down everything you typically do in a day from the time you wake up until you go to bed. Now commit to a day when you'll do none of those things. Today, remember you are a human being, not a human doing, and give up your to-do list. Now, pick one day that will look different than the rest and commit to it.

Day 15

Every good invitation does not require your acceptance. Think of all the things on the horizon for the coming month – work stuff, family stuff, birthday parties, meetings – and get it all out on paper, take a close look and start cutting back. Ask yourself: Do I really want to go there, do that, spend my energy with this group? If the answer isn't "hell, yes" then scratch it off the list. Today, decide to do things that set your soul on fire, and stop operating like your hair is on fire. Give up the need to be everywhere all the time.

Day 16

Busy work is the enemy of fulfilling work. You don't want to be busy. You want to be full. Today, imagine how you'd feel doing work that left you exhausted in the best way possible, and give up being busy.

Day 17

Today, thank someone who has supported and believed in you. Be specific about what you appreciate about them, and let them know how they have impacted your life. Give up putting off appreciation.

Day 18

Play at least one song that makes you want to sing and dance uncontrollably – and then sing and dance uncontrollably. Move your body, suspend judgment and let the music play! Today, give up small moves.

Day 19

Give up being right. Allow yourself to be true.

Day 20

From the moment you wake up until you go to bed, find 20 things that you're grateful for today. Write them down. Today, notice how you feel when you look for the good, and give up any temptation to dwell on the bad.

Day 21

Get naked. That's right, naked. Take your clothes off and stand in front of a mirror. This is the body that has carried you this far. Find one thing that you love about your naked self and take a moment to appreciate the amazing things your body has carried you through. Stand tall. Today, give up those clothes, and remember that every curve, scar, and beat of your heart serves a purpose.

Day 22

Perfect is nice, and it is also incredibly uninteresting. Today, make a mistake. In fact, make tons of them. Go screw something up, and then pay close attention to all you've learned. Do that over and over again. You have permission to be perfectly imperfect. Today, give up perfection.

Day 23

Pretend you don't have to go to work tomorrow or the day after that or the day after that. What will you do? How would you fill up 24 hours if a paycheck, health insurance, the mortgage and the 401(k) could be placed on hold for a minute? Today, imagine that you can decide exactly how you fill the next 24 hours, and write it down. Give up the notion that your safety net is safe.

Day 24

Leave the office on time. The extra hour in the office is an hour that could be spent on you. Hours add up. Today, there is no "one more thing and then I'll leave." You made the most of your time; now it's time to go home. Today, give up a late night at the office.

Day 25

The great mysteries of life should not include your current financial situation. Money is a current. It can either wash us out or we can direct the flow. Today, put a plan in place to reveal any mystery around the dollars you have. Know what you have, and allocate it appropriately. Give up the money mystery.

Day 26

Authentically wonder. Wonder what would happen if you started taking steps in the direction of your dream. Wonder what would happen if you didn't. Today, do one thing that moves you toward the life you dream of living, and give up avoiding your imagination.

Day 27

Make immediate decisions today. If someone asks what you need, tell them. If they don't ask and you need something, speak up. Tossing around ideas with friends about where to grab lunch? You make the decision and get the group on the road. Today give up the urge to let others decide where you'll go and what you'll do. If you need something, ask for it. Today, you decide.

Day 28

Give up the normal route. Today, wander.

Day 29

Write a resignation letter. What in your life is no longer serving you? Is it a thought or a belief? Is it a relationship or a habit? Today, say goodbye to at least one thing that is blocking your growth. Write it down. Say goodbye, give it up and tear it up.

Day 30

Put down the phone before you pick up the fork. Push away from the desk, and separate workspace from dining space. A time to work. A time to dine. Today, give up a working lunch.

Day 31

Stop letting someone else write your story. Each moment is a blank sheet. Don't like how the story is being told? Today, stay in your power and decide how you'll fill the page. Give up letting others author a story that can only be written by you.

Day 32

Be ready to receive. Believe you are worthy. Believe amazing things can happen for you. Any chatter that says you are undeserving of everything good has to be silenced. Today, agree to accept the good that comes your way, and give up the urge to refuse good gifts.

Day 33

Relate. You are not alone. You are not the only one who believes there is something more, something else, a thing that you're here to do. Today, find your tribe or begin creating one, and give up any notion that no one else shares your feelings.

Day 34

You're the right age. You're not too old or too young. It's not too early or too late. Remove that dialogue from your story now. Today, trust that you are the perfect age to experiment with following the desires of your heart. Give up any belief that this is not the right time.

Day 35

What if it's not hard? What if the thing that you are talking yourself out of is an opportunity to learn more about who you truly are and holds a joy that you've never known? When did you start believing that this thing had to be hard? Today, believe you'll find ease in exploring your calling, and give up thinking it's going to be hard.

Day 36

You have permission to feel how you feel. Yes, things could be worse. They could also be better. What we need is your story without you comparing it to others. There's healing there; there's hope there. Today, own all you feel, and give up comparing yourself to others.

Day 37

Laugh. Hard. What's the one thing that makes you laugh no matter how many times you watch it, talk about it or think about it? Whatever it is, revisit it. Laughing has an immediate impact on our mood. Create space for tears of joy today, and give up any concerns about what people will think when you laugh so hard you snort.

Day 38

Surrender. You're going to reach a point when it looks like things may not work out. You may even want to quit. Learn the difference between quitting and surrendering. When you are most frustrated, when you can't see a way, when you've done all you know to do -- give up control and surrender.

Day 39

Thank someone who let you go. This doesn't mean you have to actually contact them. It does mean you have to take the time to realize that in the letting go you have been put in position for something greater. Today, give up a tie that's holding you back.

Day 40

Begin. Create. What is the thing that won't leave you alone until you create it? Do not fast forward to the end and how you think it will be received if you put it out in the world. Create it now, today. Begin. Today, give up delay.

Made in the USA
Middletown, DE
31 August 2018